LOS GATOS LIBRARY

LOS GATOS, CALIFORNIA

D0710715

LOS GATOS LIBRARY

LOS GATOS, CALIFORNIA

ARCHITECTURE & CONSTRUCTION

Exploring Career Pathways

Diane Lindsey Reeves

Created and produced by
Bright Futures Press, Cary, North Carolina
www.brightfuturespress.com

Published by
Cherry Lake Publishing, Ann Arbor, Michigan
www.cherrylakepublishing.com

Photo Credits Cover, BeautyLine; page 7, Microgen; tektur, Shestakoff, Chad McDermott, Dariush M, zstock, Kaspars Grinvalds, Linda Macpherson; page 8, Kaspars Grinvalds; page 10, Shestakoff; page 12, Linda McPherson; page 14, Dariush M; page 16, Microgen; page 18, tektur; page 20, zstock; page 22, Chad McDermott; page 24, smileus.

Copyright @ 2017 by Bright Futures Press

All rights reserved. No part of this book may be reproduced or utilized in any form or by any means without written permission from the publisher.

Library of Congress Cataloging-in-Publication Data

Names: Reeves, Diane Lindsey, 1959- author.
Title: Architecture & construction / Diane Lindsey Reeves.
Other titles: Architecture and construction
Description: Ann Arbor, Michigan : Cherry Lake Publishing, 2017. I Series:
   World of work I Includes bibliographical references and index.
Identifiers: LCCN 2016042178I ISBN 9781634726238 (hardcover) I ISBN
   9781634726337 (pdf) I ISBN 9781634726436 (pbk.) I ISBN 9781634726535
   (ebook)
Subjects: LCSH: Architecture--Vocational guidance--Juvenile literature. I
   Construction industry--Vocational guidance--Juvenile literature.
Classification: LCC NA1995 .R44 2017 I DDC 720.23--dc23
LC record available at https://lccn.loc.gov/2016042178

Printed in the United States of America.

TABLE OF CONTENTS

HELLO WORLD OF WORK

This is you.

Right now, your job is to go to school and learn all you can.

This is the world of work.

It's where people earn a living, find purpose in their lives, and make the world a better place.

Sooner or later, you'll have to find your way from

HERE to **THERE**.

To get started, take all the jobs in the incredibly enormous world of work and organize them into an imaginary pile. It's a big pile, isn't it? It would be pretty tricky to find the perfect job for you among so many options.

No worries!

Some very smart career experts have made it easier to figure out. They sorted jobs and industries into groups by the types of skills and products they share. These groups are called career clusters. They provide pathways that will make it easier for you to find career options that match your interests.

Architecture & Construction

Arts & Communications

Business & Administration

Education & Training

Finance

Food & Natural Resources

Government

Health Sciences

Hospitality & Tourism

Human Services

Information Technology

Law & Public Safety

Manufacturing

Marketing

Science, Technology, Engineering & Mathematics (STEM)

Transportation

Good thing you are still a kid.

You have lots of time to explore ideas and imagine yourself doing all kinds of amazing things. The **World of Work** (WoW for short) series of books will help you get started.

TAKE A HIKE!

There are 16 career pathways waiting for you to explore. The only question is: Which one should you explore first?

Is **Architecture and Construction** a good path for you to start exploring career ideas? There is a lot to like about careers in this pathway. **Creativity** is a big part of many **architecture** and **construction** professions. In many cases, these professionals get the opportunity to see their ideas turned into reality. Their work results in new homes, bridges, parks, skyscrapers, highways, and more.

See if any of the following questions grab your interest.

WOULD YOU ENJOY making things with LEGOs, building a treehouse or birdhouse, or designing the world's best skate park?

CAN YOU IMAGINE someday working at a construction site, a design firm, or a building company?

ARE YOU CURIOUS ABOUT what civil engineers, demolition engineers, heavy equipment operators, landscape architects, or urban planners do?

If so, it's time to take a hike! Keep reading to see what kinds of opportunities you can discover along the Architecture and Construction pathway.

But wait!

What if you don't think you'll like this pathway?

You have two choices.

You could keep reading, to find out more than you already know. You might be surprised to learn how many amazing careers you'll find along this path.

OR

Turn to page 27 to get ideas about other WoW pathways.

HEAVY EQUIPMENT OPERATOR

PRESERVATIONIST

DEMOLITION ENGINEER

WoW Up Close

Building bridges and skyscrapers. Developing homes and communities for people to enjoy living in. Driving heavy equipment at construction sites. These are just some of the important jobs that people who work along the Architecture and Construction pathway do.

CIVIL ENGINEER

GENERAL CONTRACTOR

URBAN PLANNER

ARCHITECT

SOLAR ENERGY TECHNICIAN

ARCHITECT

You enjoy the work of architects every day. An **architect** designed the house you live in, the school you attend, the place where you worship, and the stores you frequent. They even design the sports stadiums where you cheer on your favorite teams! Architects imagine and design all the places where people live, work, and play.

Architecture is a mix of art and science. Anyone can imagine a building with four walls and a roof. It takes creative talent and strong science and math skills to design buildings that have both form and function. Form is the way a building looks. Function is the way it performs. For example, an architect is successful when he or she designs homes that are beautiful to look at and comfortable to live in.

Architects start with ideas to create new structures. Ideas for the world's tallest skyscraper might start out as scribbled sketches in an architect's notepad. Then the architect plans out every possible detail for how to turn those ideas into an actual skyscraper where thousands of people will visit and work. Technology like **computer-aided design** allows architects to create the extremely detailed plans that builders and **engineers** will use to construct the structure.

Frequent visits to job sites are also part of an architect's job. That's where they see their ideas turned into reality.

Check It Out!

See what you can find out about architecture at

 http://www.archKIDecture.org

Start Now!

- Create a chart showing features of the "world's tallest skyscrapers."

- Make a sketch of what your family's home looks like.

- Play computer games like Minecraft and SimCity to hone your architectural skills.

CIVIL ENGINEER

Think big when it comes to the types of projects that **civil engineers** design, build, supervise, and maintain. *Big* as in roads, buildings, and airports. *Big* as in tunnels, dams, and bridges. *Big* as in city and community water supply and sewage treatment.

There is actually a big word that describes the types of projects civil engineers work on. The word is infrastructure. It means the kinds of systems that make businesses, cities, and nations work. Transportation, communication, sewage, water, and electrical systems are examples. When these kinds of systems work well, communities thrive and life is good.

Most of all, civil engineers are problem solvers. They use strong math skills and apply science knowledge to come up with very complex solutions. Take building a bridge. The basic problem is to get vehicles from one side of a body of water to another. But there are many other factors to consider, such as safety concerns, changing weather conditions, and volume of traffic.

Millions of people will eventually use that bridge (or other system) for many years. They will all be grateful for civil engineers who get the job done right. And seeing their results stand the test of time is one of the best things about being a civil engineer.

Check It Out!

To find out more about what civil engineers do, visit:

▶ http://www.asceville.org

▶ http://bit.ly/CivilEngineers

▶ http://bit.ly/EngineerFemale

Start Now!

Use online and library resources to find answers to questions like:

✔ Why are bridges so strong?

✔ How do skyscrapers stand so tall?

✔ How do highways get from here to there?

DEMOLITION ENGINEER

Let's say a state is building a new highway around one of its major cities. A great deal of planning has been done to get ready to start construction. Now there is only one thing standing in the way of progress: a really big mountain.

It's too high to build the highway over it. It's too wide to go around. The most efficient way is to go through it.

Enter the **demolition engineer**. It is his or her job to figure out how to blast through the mountain without collapsing the entire thing. No small feat. Through a series of very complex mathematical calculations, the problem solving begins. Decisions must be made about what equipment to use and where to place fuses and powerful explosives.

Finally, the big day arrives. It is time to get the job done. In a matter of seconds, everyone will know if the demolition engineer got it right. After a final safety check, he or she throws the switch and— **KABOOM!**

Besides blasting through mountains, a demolition job may call for using heavy equipment to make way for a new housing development. Or a wrecking ball might be needed to tear down a run-down skyscraper. Demolition engineers use sophisticated software and lots of special equipment to get rid of the old to make way for the new.

Check It Out!

See how building implosions work at

▶ http://bit.ly/ BuildingImplosion

Start Now!

- ✔ Get acquainted with some of the equipment that demolition experts use to get the job done: dynamite, wrecking ball, jackhammer, bulldozer, crane, and excavator. Find information online and at the library, and make a poster showing what each tool is used for.

- ✔ Play around with **physics** with games like Demolition City (http://bit.ly/DemoCity) and Angry Birds (https:// www.angrybirds.com/ games).

GENERAL CONTRACTOR

Building a house, an office building, or any structure involves lots of steps and skills. There are permits to obtain and foundations to dig. Floors to lay. Walls and roofs to build. There are electrical and plumbing systems to put in. The list goes on and on.

Someone has to keep track of all this work and order all the supplies. Someone has to schedule the workers and make sure that the work gets done right. That "someone" is called a **general contractor**. A general contractor is in charge of a building project. His or her job is to make sure that high-quality work gets done on time, on budget, and in the proper order.

It takes lots of construction experience to qualify for a job as a general contractor. There are no specific educational requirements, but general contractors who work with bigger companies often have a bachelor's degree in construction science or management. All general contractors must pass a special licensing exam and be licensed.

The job involves keeping lots of "balls" in the air at once. The GC has to manage lots of skilled craftspeople, materials, and schedules. He or she also has to keep the client happy by getting the work done on time and on budget.

Check It Out!

Watch general contractors in action on popular HGTV shows like Property Brothers and Fixer Upper. Find links to full episodes at

▶ http://www.hgtv.com

Start Now!

✓ Observe construction sites whenever and wherever you can. Take note of who does what and the special tools they use.

✓ Ask your parent to help you find out about free kids' workshops at your local Home Depot and Lowe's hardware stores.

✓ Make a poster of all the steps to build a house from start to finish.

HEAVY
EQUIPMENT
OPERATOR

Did you like to play with toy cars and trucks when you were little? Did you build entire towns out of building blocks (and yell at your little sister or brother when they destroyed them)?

Now that you are older, do you like to watch big trucks and bulldozers do their thing at construction sites? Can you see yourself behind the wheel of a backhoe, loader, dump truck, or crane?

Heavy equipment operators drive the big trucks and machines used to construct and maintain roads, bridges, airports, gas and oil pipelines, tunnels, buildings, and other structures. Some heavy equipment operators work in mines and quarries. Most work on solid ground, but some work with cranes and other heavy equipment on oil rigs and other structures located out in the middle of oceans.

Heavy equipment operators must have a high school diploma and special training to qualify for the job. Apprenticeship programs—where new workers get supervised, on-the-job experience—are how many heavy equipment operators prepare for this work. They must obtain a **commercial driver's license** and, depending on the laws of the state where they work, may need to get special **certification**.

Check It Out!

Follow some heavy equipment operators on the job at:

- ▶ http://bit.ly/HeavyEquipOp
- ▶ http://bit.ly/FemaleHEO
- ▶ http://bit.ly/MiningHEO

Start Now!

- ✓ Make your own heavy equipment memory game. Paste pictures of different kinds of construction equipment on index cards. Write the names of each type on separate index cards. Mix them up and place them facedown on a table. Then find pairs of matching pictures and names.

PRESERVATIONIST

Take an old house. It was built over 100 years ago, has a sagging porch, and the outside paint is peeling. Inside, the woodwork is a hideous green color and the kitchen is gross. Some may think it's time to tear the old place down. But a **preservationist** would see a diamond in the rough.

Preservationists look beyond the obvious decay (and bad decorating decisions). In many cases, houses like this have good "bones," lots of character, and fine craftsmanship. With careful research and lots of hard work, preservationists can restore these types of houses to their original glory. Of course, kitchens and bathrooms would be updated with the latest in modern conveniences.

Besides houses, some preservationists work on structures with historic significance, such as the U.S. Capitol. This type of work requires in-depth knowledge of both history and special construction techniques.

According to the National Park Service, **historic preservation** is a conversation with our past about our future. It provides us with opportunities to ask, "What is important in our history?" and "What parts of our past can we preserve for the future?"

Check It Out!

Explore national historic sites online at

▶ http://bit.ly/HistoricTrust

and find a famous historic house in your state at

▶ http://bit.ly/FamousHouses

Start Now!

- ✓ Visit a local historic site with your family.

- ✓ Interview older family members or friends to find out what their lives were like when they were kids.

- ✓ Put together a time capsule with items (or pictures of items) that you think people would find interesting 100 years from now.

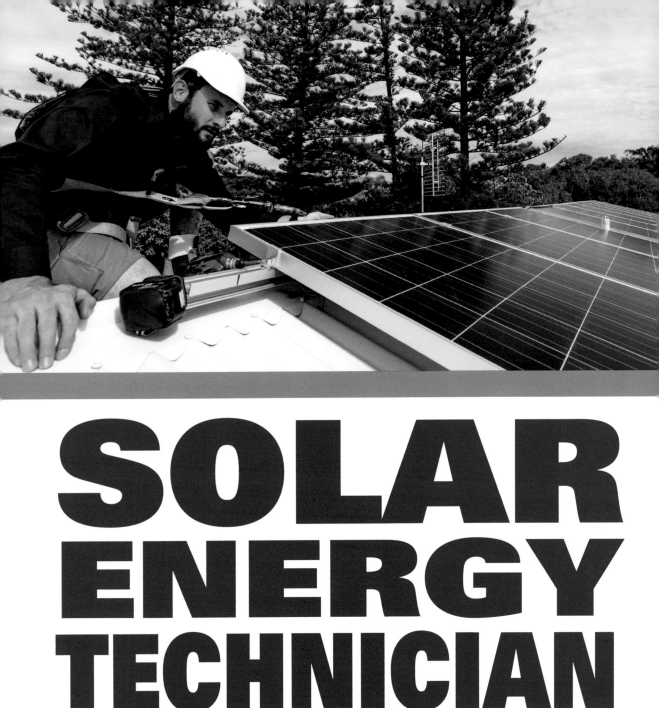

SOLAR ENERGY TECHNICIAN

According to the U.S. Department of Energy, every hour enough energy from the sun reaches Earth to meet the world's energy usage for an entire year.

So it makes sense that people are finding new ways to harness solar power as an environmentally friendly source of energy.

Solar energy technicians install solar projects in homes and businesses. This work involves special tools, safety equipment, and construction skills. Solar panels must be wired into the structure's electrical supply, so experience as an electrician helps and is sometimes required. Since the work often involves working on rooftops, those with a fear of heights need not apply!

Solar technicians called solar **photovoltaic** installers may be responsible for assembling, maintaining, or repairing panels on bigger power grids. These types of jobs are more advanced and require experience and supervision. On-the-job training is an important way that all solar energy technicians gain the skills they need to do this specialized work.

Solar energy is a growing field. There are additional opportunities in research, manufacturing, and solar power plant construction.

Check It Out!

Find out all you can about solar energy at these sites

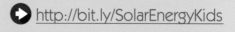 http://bit.ly/SolarEnergyKids

http://bit.ly/BillNyeSolar

Start Now!

- Go solar for your next science fair project. Research ideas online using the search terms "solar science projects for kids."

- Make a model of Earth's solar system.

- Keep a weather journal and pay special attention to what the sun is like on different types of day.

URBAN PLANNER

Urban is another word for *city*. So a simple definition of **urban planner** is someone who plans cities. And there has never been a more exciting time to be involved in planning cities of the future.

This is true because urban planners are rethinking the ways that people live and work. They are looking at better ways to move people from place to place and are coming up with creative new transportation systems. Making cities good places to live, work, and play is what urban planning is all about.

There is a lot of buzz about "sustainable" and "green" cities. Finding smarter ways to use and save energy is important to urban planners. Their job is to figure out the best way to use land and space within a city. They may also help design parks, greenways, and urban gardens. The goal is to create places that are both people- and Earth-friendly.

Urban planners tend to work for government agencies or real estate development companies in larger towns or cities. It takes a master's degree from college to become an urban planner.

In many cases, urban planners are going "back to the future." They look at the way big cities were originally built with houses, businesses, and shopping mixed together. They now created mixed used developments that make it easier to get from one place to another.

Check It Out!

Design an Earth-friendly city of the future at

 http://www.planitgreenlive. com

Start Now!

- ✓ Make a list of the 10 best things about the city where you live.

- ✓ Draw a map of your route from home to school. What kinds of places do you pass along the way?

- ✓ Create a collage showing your ideas for a cool place where kids could hang out after school.

ARCHITECT • Backhoe operator • Boilermaker • Brick mason • Building foreman • Building inspector • Bulldozer operator • Cabinetmaker • Carpenter • Carpet installer • Cartographer • Ceiling tile installer • Cement mason • Civil drafter • CIVIL ENGINEER • Code official • Computer-aided design (CAD) drafter • Concrete finisher • Construction laborer • Construction manager • Construction worker • Cost estimator • Crane operator • DEMOLITION ENGINEER • Drafter • Dredge operator • Drywall installer • Earth driller • Electrical engineer • Electrician • Electromechanical equipment assembler • Elevator inspector • Elevator

WoW Big List

Take a look at some of the different kinds of jobs people do in the Architecture and Construction pathway. **WoW!**

Some of these job titles will be familiar to you. Others will be so unfamiliar that you will scratch your head and say "huh?"

installer • Elevator repairer • Environmental designer • Environmental engineer • Excavator • Explosives worker • Fence erector • Field supervisor • Floor finisher • Floor layer • Gardener • GENERAL CONTRACTOR • Geothermal technician • Glazier • Hazardous materials removal worker • Heating, air-conditioning, and refrigeration mechanic • HEAVY EQUIPMENT OPERATOR • Highway maintenance worker • Hoist and winch operator • Home appliance repair person • Industrial engineer • Insulation worker • Interior designer • Ironworker • Landscape architect • Landscaper • Loader operator • Maintenance worker • Manufacturer's representative • Materials engineer • Mechanical drafter • Mechanical engineer • Metal fabricator • Millwright • Modeler • Painter • Paper hanger • Paving equipment operator • Photogrammetrist • Pipefitter • Plasterer • **PRESERVATIONIST** • Project manager • Refractory materials repairer • Remodeler • Restoration technician • Rigger • Roofer • Safety director • Scheduler • Security system and alarm installer • Septic tank servicer •

Find a job title that makes you curious. Type the name of the job into your favorite Internet search engine and find out more about the people who have that job.

 1 What do they do?

2 Where do they work?

3 How much training do they need to do this job?

Service contractor • Sewer pipe cleaner • Sheet metal worker • **SOLAR ENERGY TECHNICIAN** • Solar photovoltaic installer • Steelworker • Stone mason • Superintendent • Surveyor • Taper • Terrazzo finisher • Thermal contractor • Truck driver • **URBAN PLANNER** • Utility metering technician • Wastewater maintenance technician • Weatherization technician • Welder • Wind turbine service technician • Woodworker

	Put stars next to your 3 favorite career ideas	Put an X next to the career idea you like the least	Put a question mark next to the career idea you want to learn more about
Architect			
Civil Engineer			
Demolition Engineer			
General Contractor			
Heavy Equipment Operator			
Preservationist			
Solar Energy Technician			
Urban Planner			
	What do you like most about these careers?	What is it about this career that doesn't appeal to you?	What do you want to learn about this career? Where can you find answers?
	Which Big Wow List ideas are you curious about?		

Please do **NOT** write in this book if it doesn't belong to you. You can download a copy of this activity online at www.cherrylakepublishing.com/activities.

EXPLORE SOME MORE

The Architecture and Construction pathway is only one of 16 career pathways that hold exciting options for your future. Take a look at the other 15 to figure out where to start exploring next.

Arts & Communications

WOULD YOU ENJOY drawing your own cartoons, using your smartphone to make a movie, or writing articles for the student newspaper?

CAN YOU IMAGINE someday working at a Hollywood movie studio, a publishing company, or a television news station?

ARE YOU CURIOUS ABOUT what actors, bloggers, graphic designers, museum curators, or writers do?

Business & Administration

WOULD YOU ENJOY playing Monopoly, being the boss of your favorite club or team, or starting your own business?

CAN YOU IMAGINE someday working at a big corporate headquarters, government agency, or international business center?

ARE YOU CURIOUS ABOUT what brand managers, chief executive officers, e-commerce analysts, entrepreneurs, or purchasing agents do?

Education & Training

WOULD YOU ENJOY babysitting, teaching your grandparents how to use a computer, or running a summer camp for neighbor kids in your backyard?

CAN YOU IMAGINE someday working at a college counseling center, corporate training center, or school?

ARE YOU CURIOUS ABOUT what animal trainers, coaches, college professors, guidance counselors, or principals do?

Finance

WOULD YOU ENJOY earning and saving money, being the class treasurer, or playing the stock market game?

CAN YOU IMAGINE someday working at an accounting firm, bank, or Wall Street stock exchange?

ARE YOU CURIOUS ABOUT what accountants, bankers, fraud investigators, property managers, or stockbrokers do?

 Food & Natural Resources

WOULD YOU ENJOY exploring nature, growing your own garden, or setting up a recycling center at your school?

CAN YOU IMAGINE someday working at a national park, raising crops in a city farm, or studying food in a laboratory?

ARE YOU CURIOUS ABOUT what landscape architects, chefs, food scientists, environmental engineers, or forest rangers do?

Government

WOULD YOU ENJOY reading about U.S. presidents, running for student council, or helping a favorite candidate win an election?

CAN YOU IMAGINE someday working at a chamber of commerce, government agency, or law firm?

ARE YOU CURIOUS about what mayors, customs agents, federal special agents, intelligence analysts, or politicians do?

Health Sciences

WOULD YOU ENJOY nursing a sick pet back to health, dissecting animals in a science lab, or helping the school coach run a sports clinic?

CAN YOU IMAGINE someday working at a dental office, hospital, or veterinary clinic?

ARE YOU CURIOUS ABOUT what art therapists, doctors, dentists, pharmacists, and veterinarians do?

 Hospitality & Tourism

WOULD YOU ENJOY traveling, sightseeing, or meeting people from other countries?

CAN YOU IMAGINE someday working at a convention center, resort, or travel agency?

ARE YOU CURIOUS ABOUT what convention planners, golf pros, tour guides, resort managers, or wedding planners do?

Human Services

WOULD YOU ENJOY showing a new kid around your school, organizing a neighborhood food drive, or being a peer mediator?

CAN YOU IMAGINE someday working at an elder care center, fitness center, or mental health center?

ARE YOU CURIOUS ABOUT what elder care center directors, hairstylists, personal trainers, psychologists, or religious leaders do?

Information Technology

WOULD YOU ENJOY creating your own video game, setting up a Web site, or building your own computer?

CAN YOU IMAGINE someday working at an information technology start-up company, software design firm, or research and development laboratory?

ARE YOU CURIOUS ABOUT what artificial intelligence scientists, big data analysts, computer forensic investigators, software engineers, or video game designers do?

Law & Public Safety

WOULD YOU ENJOY working on the school safety patrol, participating in a mock court trial at school, or coming up with a fire escape plan for your home?

CAN YOU IMAGINE someday working at a cyber security company, fire station, police department, or prison?

ARE YOU CURIOUS ABOUT what animal control officers, coroners, detectives, firefighters, or park rangers do?

Manufacturing

WOULD YOU ENJOY figuring out how things are made, competing in a robot-building contest, or putting model airplanes together?

CAN YOU IMAGINE someday working at a high-tech manufacturing plant, engineering firm, or global logistics company?

ARE YOU CURIOUS ABOUT what chemical engineers, industrial designers, supply chain managers, robotics technologists, or welders do?

Marketing

WOULD YOU ENJOY keeping up with the latest fashion trends, picking favorite TV commercials during Super Bowl games, or making posters for a favorite school club?

CAN YOU IMAGINE someday working at an advertising agency, corporate marketing department, or retail store?

ARE YOU CURIOUS ABOUT what creative directors, market researchers, media buyers, retail store managers, and social media consultants do?

Science, Technology, Engineering & Mathematics (STEM)

WOULD YOU ENJOY concocting experiments in a science lab, trying out the latest smartphone, or taking advanced math classes?

CAN YOU IMAGINE someday working in a science laboratory, engineering firm, or research and development center?

ARE YOU CURIOUS ABOUT what aeronautical engineers, ecologists, statisticians, oceanographers, or zoologists do?

Transportation

WOULD YOU ENJOY taking pilot or sailing lessons, watching a NASA rocket launch, or helping out in the school carpool lane?

CAN YOU IMAGINE someday working at an airport, mass transit system, or shipping port?

ARE YOU CURIOUS ABOUT what air traffic controllers, flight attendants, logistics planners, surveyors, and traffic engineers do?

MY WoW

I am here.

Name _____

Grade _____

School _____

Who I am.

Make a word collage! Use 5 adjectives to form a picture that describes who you are.

Where I'm going.

The next career pathway I want to explore is

_____

Some things I need to learn first to succeed.

1 _____

2 _____

3 _____

My Career Choice

To get here.

Please do **NOT** write in this book if it doesn't belong to you. You can download a copy of this activity online at www.cherrylakepublishing.com/activities.

GLOSSARY

architect
person who designs buildings and supervises the way they are built

architecture
all the jobs involved in the art or science of designing and creating buildings

certification
a way to confirm, by way of an exam or assessment, that someone has specific knowledge or skills

civil engineer
person who designs and maintains roads, bridges, dams, and other structures

commercial driver's license
a driver's license required to operate large or heavy vehicles

computer-aided design
the process of creating plans and drawings on a computer to develop the design of something, such as a home, building, or vehicle

construction
all the jobs involved in the art, trade, or work of building structures

creativity
the process of using imagination to think of new ideas

demolition engineer
person who places and detonates explosives for the purpose of demolishing structures in construction projects

engineers
people who design and create large structures (such as roads and bridges) or new products or systems by using scientific methods

general contractor
person responsible for the overall coordination and management of a construction project

heavy equipment operator
person who operates heavy equipment, trucks, and machinery used in construction and engineering projects

historic preservation
an endeavor that seeks to preserve, conserve, and protect buildings, objects, landscapes, or other artifacts of historical significance

photovoltaic
relating to the production of electric current at the junction of two substances exposed to light

physics
the branch of science concerned with the nature and properties of matter and energy

preservationist
person who works to preserve or restore buildings or historic sites

solar energy technician
person who installs and ensures the efficient functioning of equipment that collects, generates, and distributes solar power

urban planner
person who plans and designs public, commercial, and residential spaces in cities

INDEX

* Refers to the Web page sources

About the Author

Diane Lindsey Reeves is the author of lots of children's books. She has written several original PEANUTS stories (published by Regnery Kids and Sourcebooks). She is especially curious about what people do and likes to write books that get kids thinking about all the cool things they can be when they grow up. She lives in Cary, North Carolina, and her favorite thing to do is play with her grandkids—Conrad, Evan, Reid, and Hollis Grace.